MW01251799

AND
SHELLFISH
FRIENDS

By
Sherri Eldridge

Illustrations by
Rob Groves

Lobster and Shellfish Friends

Published by:
Harvest Hill Press
P.O. Box 55
Salisbury Cove, Maine 04672
207-288-8900

ISBN: 1-886862-20-6

First printing: June 1997
Second printing: August 1998

PRINTED IN THE UNITED STATES
ON ACID-FREE PAPER

The recipes in this book were created with the goal of reducing fat, calories, cholesterol and sodium. They also present a variety of fresh healthy foods, to be prepared with love and eaten with pleasure.

CREDITS:

Cover: Cotton print border gratefully used as a courtesy of:
          Hoffman California Fabrics, Inc.

Cover Design, Layout and Typesetting: Sherri Eldridge

Front Cover Watercolor and Text Line Art: Robert Groves

Text Typesetting and Proofreading: Bill Eldridge

PREFACE

Until recently, shellfish was forbidden to people on low cholesterol diets. After extensive research, we now know that the type of cholesterol and fats found in fish and shellfish do not raise, but actually lower cholesterol levels! That makes shellfish a heart-healthy choice.

Shellfish are divided into two classes: crustaceans and mollusks. Crustaceans are sea animals with hard-crusted bodies that are segmented and joined together by flexible membranes. Mollusks are aquatic animals characterized by a hard shell of one or two pieces that encompass a soft body. Mollusks are further divided into two classes: univalves (one valve) and bivalves (two valves).

Crustaceans include the American or Maine lobster, crayfish including the rock and spiny lobsters, crabs, and shrimp. Crabs and shrimp are found in varying sizes and varieties along all our coastal waters.

Univalve mollusks include conch, snail and squid. Bivalves include clams, oysters, mussels and scallops. East Coast clams are primarily quahog, steamer and surf. On the West Coast there are over 34 varieties. Mussels are consumed in abundance in Europe, and are starting to make inroads in U.S. markets.

CONTENTS

Crab and Swiss Omelette

1 fresh asparagus stalk,
    cut into ½-inch pieces
1 tablespoon fresh crab meat
1 tablespoon white wine
1 egg
1 egg white
1 teaspoon water
fresh ground pepper
1 tablespoon grated lowfat
    Swiss cheese

Note:
Have a spatula handy
to assist in forming the
omelette . An omelette
cooks in just 30 seconds!

Serving: 1 Omelette	Calories: 125
Protein: 14 gm	Fat: 5.5 gm
Carbs: 2 gm	Cholesterol: 223 mg
Sodium: 161 mg	Calcium: 106 mg

MAKES ONE OMELETTE
Multiply ingredients by number of omelettes.

Lightly steam asparagus and crab in wine. Keep warm over low heat.

Preheat nonstick omelette pan over high heat. Whisk eggs, water and pepper together in bowl. Just before pouring eggs into pan, spray pan thoroughly with nonstick oil. Pour eggs into middle of pan (½ cup at a time if using a number of eggs). Swirl pan to distribute eggs evenly. Set on heat 5 seconds to firm the bottom while spreading asparagus, crab and grated cheese over top.

Hold pan by handle and quickly jerk toward you, while tilting far edge over burner. Continue this process and omelette will roll over on itself. When omelette forms at far end, bang on handle near pan to curl edge.

Lobster Quiche

2 tablespoons chopped onion
2 cups fresh lobster meat
1 tablespoon canola oil
1 cup sliced mushrooms
3 eggs
3 egg whites
½ lb. lowfat cottage cheese
½ teaspoon black pepper
½ teaspoon paprika
2 tablespoons chopped
   fresh parsley

Serving: 1/8 Recipe
Protein: 17 gm
Carbs: 3 gm
Sodium: 236 mg

Calories: 114
Fat: 4 gm
Cholesterol: 109 mg
Calcium: 44 mg

MAKES ONE 8-PIECE QUICHE

Preheat oven to 375°. Spray a 9-inch pie pan with nonstick oil.

Sauté onion and lobster in oil until onion is almost clear. Add mushrooms and cook 4 minutes more.

Beat 3 eggs and 2 egg whites until creamy. In a separate bowl, lightly whip single egg white, then brush it over the bottom and sides of pie plate. Blend cottage cheese into beaten eggs, thenstir in sautéed onion mixture, spices and parsley. Pour into pie plate and bake 15 minutes. Lower heat to 325° and bake 35 minutes or until quiche is firm and light brown.

Grilled Scallops with Chile Sauce

Sauce:

SERVES 4

1 cup tomato sauce
½ cup orange juice
4 tablespoons lime juice
1 teaspoon fresh grated
    ginger
2 chiles, seeded and chopped
2 tablespoons fresh cilantro
1 teaspoon onion powder
1 teaspoon garlic powder
1 teaspoon brown sugar
2 teaspoons flour

1½ lbs. large sea scallops
1 tablespoon olive oil
pinch of salt
pinch of pepper

Whisk together sauce ingredients in a saucepan. Simmer and stir over medium-high heat until thickened.

Pat and lightly squeeze scallops dry on a cloth towel. Place in bowl and toss with olive oil, salt and pepper. Thread scallops on skewers and season to taste. On a hot grill or under a broiler, cook the scallops until light brown, 2-3 minutes per side. Remove the scallops from the skewers, pour the sauce over them and serve hot.

Serving: 1/4 Recipe
Protein: 31 gm
Carbs: 20 gm
Sodium: 687 mg

Calories: 252
Fat: 5.0 gm
Cholesterol: 56 mg
Calcium: 67 mg

Colossal Crab Dip

SERVES 6

1 lb. fresh crabmeat
1 cup nonfat sour cream
8 oz. nonfat cream cheese, softened
2 teaspoons finely chopped scallions
1 tablespoon lemon juice
2 teaspoons dry sherry
dash hot pepper sauce
½ cup chopped water chestnuts
1 teaspoon paprika

Serve with
toast points or crackers

Preheat oven to 350°. Clean crabmeat, checking for shell pieces. Spray an overproof serving dish with non-stick oil.

With a whisk, whip together sour cream, cream cheese, scallions, lemon juice, sherry and hot pepper sauce. Stir in chopped water chestnuts, then crabmeat. Place in baking dish. Sprinkle with paprika. Bake 30 minutes or until bubbly. Serve this zesty dip hot or cold, with toast points or crackers for dipping.

Serving: 1/6 Recipe
Protein: 24 gm
Carbs: 12 gm
Sodium: 453 mg

Calories: 171
Fat: 2 gm
Cholesterol: 79 mg
Calcium: 204 mg

Mussels Marinière

SERVES 4

3 quarts mussels
1 tablespoon butter
3 tablespoons finely
    chopped shallots
3 tablespoons finely
    chopped celery
2 cups dry white wine
1 cup water
1 bay leaf
1 teaspoon black pepper
3 tablespoons parsley
½ cup skim milk
crusty French bread

Serving: 1/4 Recipe   Calories: 268
Protein: 22 gm   Fat: 7.0 gm
Carbs: 10 gm   Cholesterol: 56 mg
Sodium: 375 mg   Calcium: 87 mg
Nutritional analysis includes 1 loaf French bread

Scrub mussels and pull off beards. Discard any that do not close tightly when handled or have broken shells.

In a large pot, heat butter. Sauté shallots and celery until tender. Add white wine, water, bay leaf, pepper and parsley. Bring to a full boil, then add mussels. Cover pot and raise heat to high. Mussels will open and be cooked in 15 minutes.

Remove mussels with a slotted spoon. Strain broth through a fine sieve or cheesecloth and rinse out pot. Return strained broth to pot and cook down until liquid is reduced by half. Stir in milk and heat, but do not boil.

Divide mussels among serving bowls, pour sauce over mussels. Serve with crusty French bread for dipping.

The Life of a Lobster

While Maine is known for its lobster, the Homarus Americanus is caught from Labrador to North Carolina. This species has 20 pairs of gills and its first three pairs of legs are pinchers. The largest Maine lobster ever caught was 42 lbs.

The world's most popular lobster is not even a lobster, it's called a spiny or rock lobster and is actually a crayfish. With its oversized tail filled with meat, it is found off the Florida and California coasts, though many frozen spiny lobster tails are imported from Australia, South Africa and Brazil.

If purchasing fresh lobster, be sure the lobster is alive. Never cook a lobster that is already dead, it will make you very sick. When shipping live lobsters, keep them cool by packing in freezer packs, and moist seaweed if available. Lobsters can also be stored in the refrigerator for a day or two. Before cooking, lobsters are dark greenish-blue in color with specks of coral. After cooking, they will be bright red.

Steaming lobsters will best preserve their fresh taste. Fill the bottom of a large pot with 1-inch sea or salted water, cover and bring to a boil. Drop the lobsters into the pot, cover pot and cook 20 minutes for 1-1¼ pound lobsters, 30 minutes for 2+ pound lobsters. Enjoy!

Lobster Stew

1 ¼ lbs. lobster meat
2 teaspoons butter
4 cups skim milk blended
    with 1 cup nonfat
    powdered milk
1 teaspoon pepper

SERVES 4

Cut lobster meat into bite-sized pieces and sauté in butter. Add remaining ingredients and heat well for 10 minutes, but do not boil.

Serving: 1/4 Recipe
Protein: 44 gm
Carbs: 23 gm
Sodium: 780 mg

Calories: 307
Fat: 3.5 gm
Cholesterol: 115 mg
Calcium: 610 mg

New England Clam Chowder

12 large quahog or
   36 littleneck clams
2 cups boiling water
1 medium-sized onion,
   finely chopped
1 teaspoon butter
2 cups peeled and diced
   potatoes
1 teaspoon oregano
1 teaspoon basil
1 teaspoon black pepper
3 cups skim milk blended
   with 1½ cups nonfat
   powdered milk

Serving: 1/4 Recipe   Calories: 405
Protein: 40 gm   Fat: 3.5 gm
Carbs: 52 gm   Cholesterol: 68 mg
Sodium: 351 mg   Calcium: 652 mg

SERVES 4

Scrub clams, discarding any that do not close. Steam in boiling water for 20 minutes. Strain clam juice through fine sieve and reserve juice.

Sauté onion in butter. Add potatoes, milk, spices and 1 cup reserved clam juice. Simmer until potatoes are tender.

Shuck clams and coarsely chop meat. When potatoes are cooked, add clams and spices, then cook 10 minutes longer. Adjust seasonings, serve hot.

Lobster Bisque

2 live lobsters, weighing
   1-1½ lbs. each
3 cups water
1 cup peeled and diced
   potatoes
1 cup skim milk
1 tablespoon grated onion
1 clove garlic, minced
¼ cup chopped celery
¼ cup chopped carrots
½ cup Madeira
1 cup white wine
1 tablespoon tomato paste
2 tablespoons flour
2 teaspoons butter
¼ teaspoon salt
¼ teaspoon pepper

Serving: 1/6 Recipe   Calories: 164
Protein: 12 gm   Fat: 2.0 gm
Carbs: 13 gm   Cholesterol: 52 mg
Sodium: 294 mg   Calcium: 89 mg

SERVES 6

On high heat, boil water to steam lobsters and potatoes in covered pot for 25 minutes. Remove lobsters and continue cooking potatoes. Pick out lobster meat, cut into small pieces. When potatoes are tender, drain, but reserve liquid.

In a saucepan, heat milk with onion, garlic, celery and carrots. Simmer, without boiling, for 25 minutes. Strain milk into blender, add Madeira, wine, tomato paste, potatoes, 1 cup reserved liquid and ½ cup lobster meat. While blender is running, add flour. Process until smooth.

Return bisque to pot, cook until thickened, but do not boil. Stir in remaining lobster meat, butter, salt and pepper. Heat thoroughly before serving, but do not boil.

Spanish Shrimp Soup

¾ cup finely chopped onion
½ cup finely chopped green
    pepper
1 tablespoon olive oil
½ teaspoon garlic powder
½ teaspoon dried thyme
2 pinches cayenne
¼ teaspoon white pepper
1 lb. peeled, deveined and
    cooked shrimp
3 cups fish broth
4 cups hot boiled rice

SERVES 4

In a large pot, sauté onion and pepper in oil until onion is clear. Stir in spices. Chop shrimp into small pieces and mix in. Cook over medium-high heat 5 minutes.

Pour in broth and bring to a simmer. Lower heat and cook 10 minutes. Serve soup hot, ladled over hot boiled rice.

Serving: 1/4 Recipe
Protein: 32 gm
Carbs: 50 gm
Sodium: 839 mg

Calories: 398
Fat: 6.5 gm
Cholesterol: 222 mg
Calcium: 127 mg

How to Eat Lobster and Clams

Lobster: Bend back claws and flippers, and break off where attached to the body. Use crackers and pick to crack the claws and knuckles. Remove meat and suck meat from small flippers.

Bend back tail and break off from body. Tail flippers can also be broken back and the tail meat pushed out, or you can cut the membrane. In the body is the green tomalley (liver) and red coral of the females (roe).

Clams: Wedge open shells and loosen meat. Dip in broth to rinse off sand.

Oriental Crab Salad

4 cups fresh crabmeat
2 cups cucumbers, peeled,
   halved, seeded and
   thinly sliced
2 cups shredded cabbage
2 tablespoons grated red
   onion
2 tablespoons sesame seeds
¼ cup minced cilantro
1 cup rice vinegar
1 tablespoon honey
2 tablespoons fresh grated
   gingerroot
2 tablespoons soy sauce
1 tablespoon sesame oil
pinch of salt
¼ cup macadamia nuts
1 cup chow mein noodles
Garnish with:
lettuce leaves, tomato slices

SERVES 10

In a large bowl, combine crabmeat, cucumbers, cabbage, onion, sesame seeds and cilantro. In another bowl, whisk vinegar, honey, gingerroot, soy sauce, oil and salt. Pour over crab mixture, add nut and noodles, toss well.

Line a platter with lettuce and sliced tomato rounds. Mound Oriental Crab Salad on platter, and serve cold.

Serving: 1/10 Recipe
Protein: 13 gm
Carbs: 8 gm
Sodium: 299 mg

Calories: 155
Fat: 7.0 gm
Cholesterol: 55 mg
Calcium: 90 mg

White Clam Sauce and Shells

SERVES 4

2 tablespoons chopped
   shallots
2 teaspoons minced garlic
2 tablespoons olive oil
3 tablespoons chopped
   parsley
pinch of red pepper flakes
2 teaspoons all-purpose flour
1 cup white wine
½ cup clam juice
¾ cup canned or fresh
   steamed clams, rinsed
   and minced
1 teaspoon butter
3 tablespoons lowfat grated
   Parmesan cheese
8 oz. dry medium shells

Sauté shallots and garlic in olive oil. Add parsley and red pepper flakes. Whisk in flour, then white wine and clam juice. Simmer until liquid is reduced by half.

Stir in clams. Remove from heat, mix in butter and Parmesan cheese. Cover pan and place on very low heat.

Boil pasta shells until tender. Drain well. Divide among dinner plates and spoon white clam sauce on top.

Serving: 1/4 Recipe   Calories: 347
Protein: 9 gm   Fat: 10 gm
Carbs: 45 gm   Cholesterol: 8 mg
Sodium: 246 mg   Calcium: 73 mg

Fettuccine Alfredo with Scallops and Baby Peas

2 lbs. medium-sized sea
    scallops, ¾-inch diameter
3 tablespoons paprika
1 tablespoon onion powder
2 teaspoons garlic powder
2 teaspoons cumin
1 teaspoon cayenne
1 tablespoon safflower oil
2 pkgs. fresh, refrigerated
    fettuccine noodles
¼ cup skim milk blended
    with ¾ cup nonfat
    powdered milk
1½ cups grated Parmesan
    cheese
1½ cups fresh or frozen
    baby peas
1 teaspoon black pepper

SERVES 6

Rinse scallops in a colander, and pat dry on cotton towel. In a small, sturdy paper bag, combine spices. Place half of the scallops in the paper bag and shake well. Pick out scallops, and shake remaining scallops in spice bag.

Heat a cast-iron frying pan on high heat. Lightly spray with nonstick oil, and heat oil in pan. Pan-blacken scallops on both sides.

Boil noodles in a large quantity of water. Drain. Add milk and Parmesan a little at a time, tossing after each addition. Stir in scallops and peas. Heat, season with pepper, and serve at once.

Serving: 1/6 Recipe
Protein: 45 gm
Carbs: 38 gm
Sodium: 612 mg

Calories: 452
Fat: 12.5 gm
Cholesterol: 111 mg
Calcium: 441 mg

Red Lobster Sauce & Pasta

2 steamed lobsters
¼ cup chopped carrots
¼ cup chopped celery
½ cup chopped onion
1 tablespoon canola oil
¼ cup brandy
1½ cups vegetable broth
½ cup dry vermouth
5 plum tomatoes,
    chopped and drained
1 teaspoon tarragon
1 clove garlic, crushed
1 teaspoon black pepper
5 drops hot pepper sauce
2 tablespoons flour
3 tablespoons skim milk
2 tablespoons tomato paste
1 lb. dry spaghetti pasta

SERVES 4

Remove meat from lobster, chop into small pieces, and empty out the shells. Sauté the empty lobster shells, carrots, celery and onion in oil and brandy for 5 minutes. Add broth, vermouth, tomatoes, tarragon, garlic, pepper and pepper sauce. Simmer 30 minutes. Strain sauce into another saucepan, pressing juices out of the ingredients. Rapidly boil down to make about 2 cups of sauce, then remove from heat.

Combine flour, milk and tomato paste. Whisk into the sauce, then stir in lobster meat. Return to heat, stir and simmer 3 minutes. Correct seasonings to taste.

Boil pasta in slightly salted water until tender. Drain. Serve lobster sauce over hot pasta.

Serving: 1/4 Recipe	Calories: 646
Protein: 32 gm	Fat: 7.0 gm
Carbs: 97 gm	Cholesterol: 73 mg
Sodium: 296 mg	Calcium: 93 mg

Oyster Stuffing

3 tablespoons chopped onion
1 teaspoon garlic, minced
1 cup fresh chopped celery
¼ cup fresh chopped parsley
1 tablespoon butter
1 tablespoon canola oil
1 pint fresh shucked oysters
4 cups breadcrumbs

SERVES 8

Sauté onion, garlic, celery and parsley in butter and canola oil.

Chop the oysters and stir into the sauté. Cook briefly, then mix in breadcrumbs. Season to taste.

Serving: 1/8 Recipe
Protein: 7 gm
Carbs: 16 gm
Sodium: 296 mg

Calories: 143
Fat: 5.5 gm
Cholesterol: 37 mg
Calcium: 66 mg

Crab Creole

SERVES 4

1 tablespoon canola oil
4 tablespoons flour
1½ cups vegetable broth
1 cup chopped onion
1 cup chopped green pepper
1 tablespoon canola oil
3 tablespoons dry sherry
3 cups chopped peeled
   tomatoes and juice
1 bay leaf
1 teaspoon brown sugar
½ teaspoon cayenne
¼ teaspoon salt
¼ teaspoon pepper
1 lb. crab meat
4 cups hot boiled rice

Serving: 1/4 Recipe
Protein: 15 gm
Carbs: 72 gm
Sodium: 297 mg

Calories: 444
Fat: 8.5 gm
Cholesterol: 34 mg
Calcium: 78 mg

Heat 1 tablespoon of oil in a large saucepan over low heat. Make a roux by blending in flour, stirring constantly while lightly browning. Whisk in vegetable broth, and cook over medium-low heat.

In a separate saucepan, sauté onion and green pepper in another tablespoon of oil and sherry until browned. Stir in tomatoes and their juice, bay leaf, brown sugar and spices. Rapidly cook down over medium-high heat until liquid is reduced by half. Stir in flour roux, cook until thickened. Add crab meat and simmer for 5 minutes.

Remove bay leaf and serve over bed of hot boiled rice.

The Healthy Shellfish Chart

Nutritional Analysis per 3.5 oz. Raw Shellfish Meat

SHELLFISH	CALORIES	PROTEIN (GRAMS)	FAT (GRAMS)	CHOLESTEROL (MILLIGRAMS)
Clams	80	11	1.5	34
Crab, Dungeness	81	17	1.3	59
Crab, King	75	15	0.8	42
Lobster	90	17	1.9	85
Mussels	75	12	1.6	80
Oysters	70	14	1.2	55
Scallops	82	15	0.2	33
Shrimp	90	19	0.8	152

Although once restricted on low-cholesterol diets, recent research has shown the types of cholesterol in shellfish do not raise blood cholesterol levels. Fish and shellfish are heart-healthy!

The Lobster Bake Party

6 cups sea water
seaweed rinsed of sand or
    substitute leaves from
    iceberg lettuce
6 dozen steamer clams
6 lobsters, 1-1½ lbs. each
6 ears corn, husked
6 baking potatoes wrapped in
    double layers of foil

Serve with
bowls of lemon juice and
    clam juice mixed with
    pinch of salt and pepper

Bring along
corn and potato fixings
lobster crackers and picks

Serving: 1/6 Recipe
Protein: 65 gm
Carbs: 67 gm
Sodium: 621 mg

Calories: 568
Fat: 5.0 gm
Cholesterol: 218 mg
Calcium: 210 mg

SERVES 6

Preparation: Scrub clams, discarding any with broken shells or that do not close tightly when handled. Place clams by the dozen in squares of cheesecloth and tie with string. Allow room in bags for clams to open.

Dig a 3-foot-deep hole in the sand or gravel. Build a fire of driftwood. Let it die down and turn to hot coals about 2 hours before sunset. Set 24-quart steamer pot in hole over embers. Pour sea water into pot and line with 2 inches of seaweed. Place lobsters and corn in pot. Cover with 4 inches rinsed seaweed. Put clam bags on seaweed, cover pot. Place wrapped potatoes around base of pot. Fill in hole with sand or gravel, covering potatoes and pot. Leave covered about 1½ hours. Carefully dig up lobster pot and potatoes, and feast!

Dungeness Crab Cakes in Champagne Sauce

SERVES 4

Champagne Sauce:
¼ cup clam juice
1 cup dry champagne
2 shallots, chopped
¾ cup nonfat cottage cheese
½ cup lowfat buttermilk
pinch each of salt and pepper
1 tablespoon lemon juice

Crab Cakes:
3 cups fresh Dungeness (or other type) crab meat
1 egg, beaten
1 egg white, beaten
¼ cup champagne
2 teaspoons extra-virgin olive oil
¾ cup plain breadcrumbs
¼ teaspoon spiced mustard

Serving: 1/4 Recipe	Calories: 275
Protein: 31 gm	Fat: 6 gm
Carbs: 12 gm	Cholesterol: 156 mg
Sodium: 563 mg	Calcium: 162 mg

Place clam juice in pot over medium heat, add champagne and chopped shallots. Simmer 10 minutes, occasionally skimming off surface.

In a blender, whip together cottage cheese and buttermilk until completely smooth. Pour into sauce and simmer 8 minutes, or until thickened. Remove from heat, add spices and lemon juice. Cover saucepan and keep on low heat.

In a large mixing bowl, blend together crab cake ingredients reserving ¼ cup breadcrumbs. Form into patties and coat with remaining ¼ cup breadcrumbs. Spray frying pan with non-stick oil. Lightly coat with olive oil and warm on medium-high heat. Fry crab cakes on both sides, serve with Champagne Sauce spooned on top of Crab Cakes.

Lazyman's Lobster Pie

4 cups cooked lobster meat,
   cut into bite-sized pieces
2 tablespoons butter, melted
3 tablespoons vermouth
2 tablespoons chopped
   parsley
pinch of pepper
1½ cups plain breadcrumbs
1 tablespoon canola oil

Serving: 1/4 Recipe
Protein: 31 gm
Carbs: 10 gm
Sodium: 701 mg

Calories: 286
Fat: 11.0 gm
Cholesterol: 120 mg
Calcium: 115 mg

SERVES 4

Preheat oven to 350°. Spray 4 individual casserole dishes with non-stick oil.

Toss lobster meat with melted butter, vermouth, parsley and pepper. Put lobster into prepared casserole dishes.

Mix 1 cup breadcrumbs with canola oil and toss. Sprinkle remaining crumbs over lobster. Place on upper oven rack and bake until tops are lightly browned.

Shrimp Étouffé

1 tablespoon safflower oil
1 cup chopped yellow onion
1 cup chopped green pepper
2 cloves garlic, minced
4 peeled plum tomatoes,
    chopped
1 cup vegetable broth
1 cup tomato juice
1 teaspoon thyme
1 teaspoon saffron
1 bay leaf
½ teaspoon hot pepper sauce
1½ lbs. peeled, deveined
    and chopped shrimp
3 tablespoons chopped
    parsley

**Serve over
hot boiled rice**

SERVES 4

In a large skillet, heat oil, sauté onion, pepper and garlic. Add chopped tomatoes, vegetable broth, tomato juice, thyme, saffron, bay leaf and Tabasco sauce. Simmer 20 minutes or until sauce thickens.

Stir in shrimp and parsley, simmer 10 minutes. Stir, remove bay leaf, and serve immediately over hot boiled rice.

Serving: 1/4 Recipe
Protein: 37 gm
Carbs: 17 gm
Sodium: 503 mg
Calories: 280
Fat: 7.0 gm
Cholesterol: 258 mg
Calcium: 122 mg

Seafood Enchiladas

SERVES 4

Sauce:
1½ cups chopped onion
3 cloves garlic, minced
1 tablespoon canola oil
1 teaspoon cumin
1 cup nonfat sour cream
¾ cup skim milk
1 cup diced chile peppers
1 tablespoon oregano
¼ teaspoon pepper
1 small dried red chile
pepper, pulverized

Enchiladas:
½ lb. cooked bay scallops
1 cup crabmeat
½ lb. shrimp, peeled,
deveined and chopped
5 large corn tortillas
1½ cups grated jack cheese

Sauté onion and garlic in oil until onion is clear. Stir in remaining sauce ingredients. Whisk gently and slowly bring to a boil. Reduce heat and simmer 15 minutes.

Preheat oven to 400°. Assemble enchiladas: Combine seafood in a bowl. Spray a baking dish the size of the tortillas with nonstick oil. Make five layers each consisting of a tortilla, ¹/₅ of the grated cheese, ¹/₅ of the seafood mixture, and ¹/₅ of the sauce. The final layer ends with the sauce on top. Bake until the enchiladas are cooked through, about 25 minutes. Serve immediately.

Serving: 1/4 Recipe   Calories: 474
Protein: 49 gm   Fat: 12.5 gm
Carbs: 40 gm   Cholesterol: 186 mg
Sodium: 630 mg   Calcium: 575 mg

Lobster Newburg

SERVES 6

1 tablespoon butter
2 tablespoons finely
    chopped shallots
½ cup Madeira
2 cups skim milk blended
    with 1 cup nonfat
    powdered milk
2 eggs
1½ tablespoons tomato paste
pinch of white pepper
1½ lbs. cooked lobster meat
6 slices toast, halved

Heat butter in saucepan. Sauté shallots for 5 minutes. Stir in Madeira and heat.

Beat milk with eggs until creamy. Whisk into shallot mixture, stirring constantly while sauce thickens. Add tomato paste and white pepper. When thickened, gently fold in lobster and heat. Serve Lobster Newburg over sliced toast halves.

Serving: 1/6 Recipe
Protein: 34 gm
Carbs: 24 gm
Sodium: 687 mg

Calories: 293
Fat: 5.0 gm
Cholesterol: 120 mg
Calcium: 347 mg

Glorious Seafood Stew

1 leek
1 tablespoon olive oil
½ cup chopped celery
½ cup chopped onion
2 cloves garlic, minced
2 cups crushed tomatoes
1 teaspoon brown sugar
¼ cup bottled clam juice
2 cups red wine
1 teaspoon thyme
1 bay leaf
3 tablespoons chopped
    parsley
4 small lobsters
32 mussels, cleaned
1 lb. small bay scallops
1 lb. fresh fish (any kind),
    cut into small pieces
18 large shrimp, cooked,
    peeled and deveined

Serving: 1/8 Recipe
Protein: 52 gm
Carbs: 12 gm
Sodium: 616 mg

Calories: 357
Fat: 5.5 gm
Cholesterol: 208 mg
Calcium: 123 mg

SERVES 8

Wash leek well. Discard tough outer leaves and rinse again. Chop tender lower leaves and stalk.

In a large pot, heat oil and sauté celery, onion and garlic. Stir in chopped leek, tomatoes, brown sugar, clam juice, wine, spices and parsley. Simmer 30 minutes.

In a separate pot, boil lobsters for 20 minutes. Use tongs to remove lobsters. Place mussels in the boiling water until they open, about 15 minutes. Drain.

Add scallops, fish and shrimp to stew. Cook 10 minutes. Remove lobster meat from shells and cut into bite-sized pieces. Stir in lobster meat, cook 5 minutes more. Remove bay leaf and serve bowls of stew with mussels in the shell placed on top.